D1105979

DK READERS

Level 2

Level 3

A Note to Parents

DK READERS is a compelling program for beginning readers, designed in conjunction with leading literacy experts, including Dr. Linda Gambrell, Distinguished Professor of Education at Clemson University. Dr. Gambrell has served as President of the National Reading Conference, the College Reading Association, and the International Reading Association.

Beautiful illustrations and superb full-color photographs combine with engaging, easy-to-read stories to offer a fresh approach to each subject in the series. Each DK READER is guaranteed to capture a child's interest while developing his or her reading skills, general knowledge, and love of reading.

The five levels of DK READERS are aimed at different reading abilities, enabling you to choose the books that are exactly right for your child:

Pre-level 1: Learning to read
Level 1: Beginning to read
Level 2: Beginning to read alone
Level 3: Reading alone
Level 4: Proficient readers

The "normal" age at which a child begins to read can be anywhere from three to eight years old. Adult participation through the lower levels is very helpful for providing encouragement, discussing storylines, and sounding out unfamiliar words.

No matter which level you select, you can be sure that you are helping your child learn to read, then read to learn!

LONDON, NEW YORK, MUNICH,
MELBOURNE, AND DELHI

Senior Editor Helen Murray
Designer Lauren Rosier
Managing Editor Laura Gilbert
Design Manager Nathan Martin
Publishing Manager Julie Ferris
Art Director Ron Stobbart
Publishing Director Simon Beecroft
Pre-Production Producer Rebecca
Fallowfield
Producer Louise Daly

Designed and edited by Tall Tree Ltd
Designer Malcolm Parchment
Editor Catherine Saunders

Reading Consultant
Linda B. Gambrell, Ph.D.

First American Edition, 2013
10 9 8 7 6 5 4 3 2 1
Published in the United States by DK Publishing
375 Hudson Street, New York, New York 10014

LEGO and the LEGO logo are trademarks of the LEGO Group.
© 2013 the LEGO Group
Produced by Dorling Kindersley under license
from the LEGO Group.

001–187436–March/13

DK books are available at special discounts when purchased in
bulk for sales promotions, premiums, fund-raising, or
educational use.
For details, contact:
DK Publishing Special Markets
375 Hudson Street, New York, New York 10014
SpecialSales@dk.com

A catalog record for this book is available
from the Library of Congress.

ISBN: 978-1-4654-0261-5 (paperback)
ISBN: 978-1-4654-0262-2 (hardback)

Color reproduction by Alta Image
Printed and bound in China by L.Rex

Discover more at
www.dk.com
www.LEGO.com

Contents

DK READERS

BEGINNING
2
TO READ ALONE

Let's go Riding

Written by Catherine Saunders

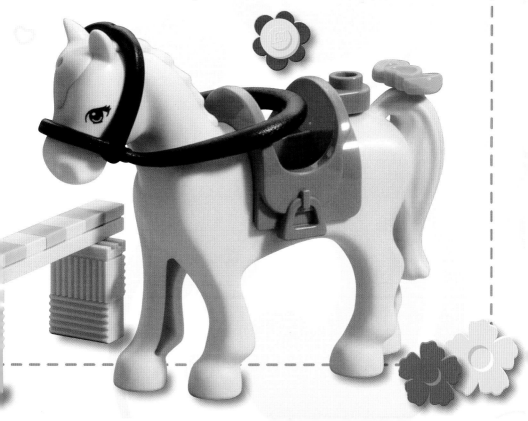

Animal friends

Olivia, Emma, Stephanie, Mia, and Andrea are best friends and they love hanging out together. The girls have many hobbies, but they share a love of animals.

Stephanie

Andrea

Puppy

Rabbit

The girls care about all animals. However, two of them share a passion for one special type of animal—horses! Come on, let's go riding with horse-crazy Mia and Emma.

Olivia

Bird

Emma

Mia

Hedgehog

Cat

Mia and Bella

Mia is an outdoor girl.
She loves camping, canoeing,
and riding her horse, Bella.
In her spare time, Mia helps the
Heartlake City vet care for sick
or injured animals.

Mane

Carrot

Beautiful Bella

Bella has a cute white stripe on her head, called a blaze. Mia thinks she's the prettiest horse in the whole world!

Bella

Mia's dream job would definitely involve animals. She might become a vet, an animal psychologist, or work in a pet rescue center.

Hay

Emma and Robin

Emma loves decorating, drawing, and designing clothes. She likes to share her talents with her friends by giving them, or their bedrooms, makeovers.

Emma dreams of becoming a fashion designer or an interior decorator one day.

Emma always seems to know what's in fashion, and what isn't. But there's one thing that will always be in fashion for Emma— her horse Robin. She thinks Robin is simply perfect.

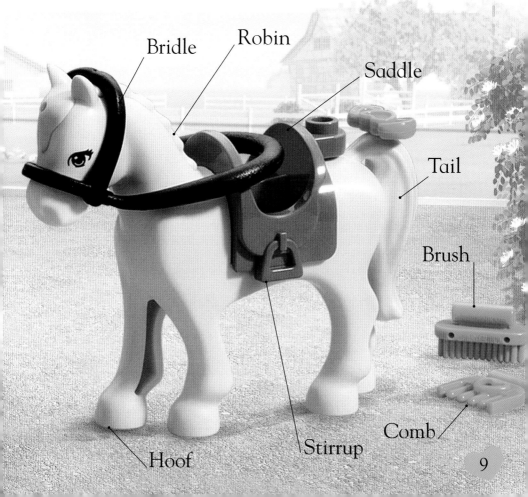

Bridle

Robin

Saddle

Tail

Brush

Comb

Stirrup

Hoof

Horse show

Emma loves horseback riding and her favorite part is jumping. Emma and Robin are a great team and they often enter horse jumping competitions.

Katharina

Gate

Today, Emma and Robin are traveling to a horse show. They plan to win the jumping contest. Emma leads Robin into his blue horse trailer. He travels in style!

Horse trailer

Ramp

Emma is getting Robin ready for the competition. First, she gives him a long drink of water and some carrots so that he has enough energy to jump high over all the fences.

Saddle

Riding hat

Riding boots

Horses love eating carrots. Robin is so gentle and friendly that Emma can feed him carrots straight from her hand.

Bridle

Reins

Next, it's time for Emma to put on her riding hat and boots. Finally, she saddles up Robin. Good luck Emma and Robin!

Emma and Robin have won
the competition! Robin cleared
all the jumps. Emma is so proud
of her clever horse.

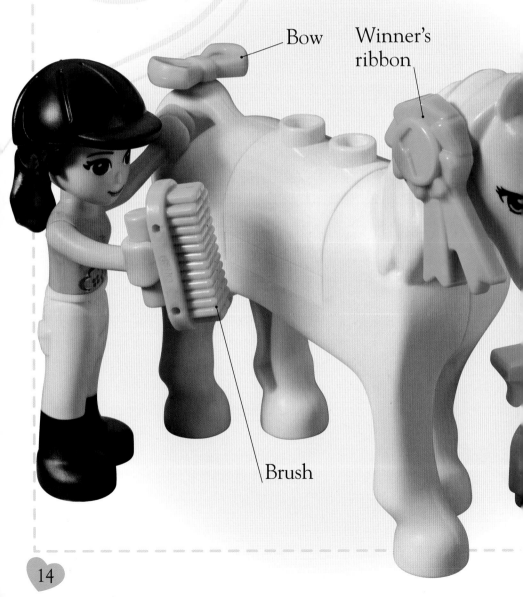

Bow

Winner's
ribbon

Brush

Jumping high
Horse jumping is hard. Emma and Robin must time their jump perfectly so they don't knock the fence down.

Emma pins the blue winner's ribbon onto Robin's mane. It's a perfect fashion accessory. Emma cleans and grooms her tired horse. Robin has worked so hard today, but now it's time to go home. Well done Robin, Emma has a special reward for you—some extra carrots!

At the stables

Mia likes to spend as much time as she can with her horse. Every day, after school, she goes to visit Bella at the stables.

Stables

Flag

Bella

Niki

Horse fan
Katharina would like to be a famous rider or a horse trainer. She has a horse called Niki.

During the school holidays, Mia can spend all day at the stables. Her friend Katharina also likes to spend a lot of time there. Mia sometimes forgets that she needs to hang out with Stephanie, Olivia, Emma, and Andrea too. Stephanie jokes that Mia prefers animals to people!

Mia brushes Bella's mane and tail every day. She also makes sure her horse has plenty of fresh hay to eat.

Looking after a horse isn't simple. Every day, Mia must feed Bella, groom her, and clean out her stable. It's hard work, but horse-loving Mia doesn't mind.

For Mia, the best part of the day is exercising Bella because that means riding her! Mia and Bella often go for very long rides.

They like to practice cantering in the beautiful countryside around Heartlake City.

Tail

Mane

Grass

It's been another busy day looking after their horses, but Mia and Katharina can finally relax. So, how do the two friends like to spend their free time?

Stable door

Flag

Bella

Niki

Mia and Katharina have spent all day with their horses, but they can't wait to come back tomorrow.

They talk about horses and read horse magazines, of course!

Bella and Niki are happy too. They've had a very exciting day thanks to Mia and Katharina.

Now the sleepy horses are safe and secure in their clean stables.

Water well

Off to the vet

Mia is worried about Bella. Something seems to be wrong with one of her front hooves. Poor Bella is limping, but Mia knows someone who can help: Sophie, the Heartlake City vet.

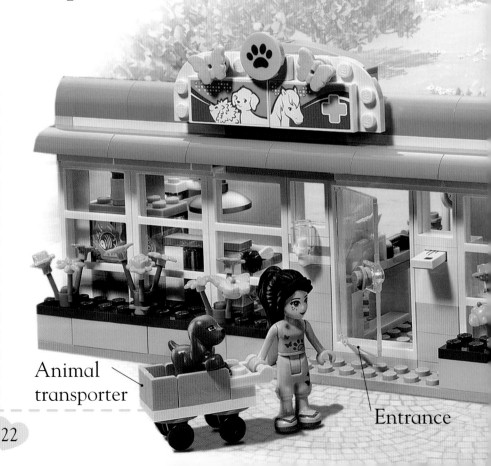

Animal transporter

Entrance

Sophie is also Mia's friend Olivia's aunt. Mia is sure that she'll know exactly what to do for Bella.

Stable

Sophie carefully checks Bella's injured hoof and immediately finds the problem. Bella has a stone in her hoof! The vet very gently removes the stone.

A rescue hedgehog

A sick puppy

Mia loves helping Sophie with the animals.
It's good practice for her future career!

Sophie gives Bella a
carrot for being such a
brave horse. Bella will be
fine now, she just needs to
rest for a while. So, Mia
stays to help Sophie with
the other animals, while
Bella recovers.

Riding camp

Stephanie also loves horses and she has an idea for the perfect summer vacation—riding camp! She invites Emma and her friend Ella to join her.

Old friend

Ella and Stephanie live in different towns, but they email, phone, text, or write to each other regularly.

Emma and Ella think it's a wonderful plan. At riding camp they'll be able to go on long horseback rides, talk about horses all day, and make lots of new, equally horse-crazy, friends. So, the three excited girls set off in their stylish minibus. Riding camp, here they come!

Theresa is an experienced riding
instructor and horse expert.

Riding camp is just as much
fun as Stephanie, Emma, and Ella
thought it would be, but it's hard
work too! Theresa, the riding
instructor, teaches the girls
how to ride horses, how
to feed them, and how
to care for them.

After their lessons, the girls practice what they have learned in the paddock. By the end of the camp, Stephanie, Emma, and Ella will be expert horse riders!

Robin

Horse cart

Theresa

It's been another fantastic day at riding camp, but Stephanie, Emma, and Ella must go home tomorrow. However, Theresa has something extra-special planned for their last night at camp.

Hot chocolate

Campfire

Marshmallow

Emma and Stephanie are too excited to sleep. They can't wait to tell Andrea, Mia, and Olivia all about riding camp!

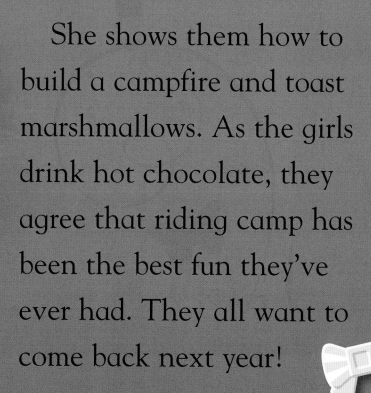

She shows them how to build a campfire and toast marshmallows. As the girls drink hot chocolate, they agree that riding camp has been the best fun they've ever had. They all want to come back next year!

Quiz

1. What color is Robin's horse trailer?

2. What is the name of Katharina's horse?

3. How do Mia and Katharina like to relax?

4. What is the name of the Heartlake City vet?

5. Who goes to riding camp with Stephanie and Emma?

1. Blue 2. Niki 3. By reading horse magazines and talking about horses 4. Sophie 5. Ella

Index

DK READERS

My name is

_____

I have read this book

Date

_____